SQUATTERS

SQUATTERS

YOU MAY BE LIVING WITH YOUR ENEMY!

KAKRA BAIDEN

Copyright © 2020 by Airpower Publishing Inc.

SQUATTERS
by Kakra Baiden

Printed in the United States of America

ISBN: 978-1-945123-21-4

All rights reserved. This book or parts thereof may not be reproduced in any form, stored in a retrieval system, or transmitted in any form by any means—electronic, mechanical, photocopy, recording, or otherwise—without prior written permission of the publisher, except as provided by United States of America copyright law.

Unless otherwise noted, all Scripture quotations are from the King James Version of the Bible.

Visit the author's website at www.kakrabaiden.org.

While the author has made every effort to provide accurate telephone numbers and Internet addresses at the time of publication, neither the publisher nor the author assumes any responsibility for errors or for changes that occur after publication.

Design Director: Bill Johnson
Cover design by Terry Clifton

To my spiritual father,
Bishop Dag Heward-Mills.
You are simply fantastic.
I thank God for all the spiritual
investments you have made in my life.
God bless you.

To my darling wife, Ewuradwoa,
and my children—Phoebe, Caleb, Joshua,
and Chloe. I thank you for your support
and sacrifice. I love you dearly.

To my parents,
Moses and Georgina Baiden.
You have been wonderful parents.

Finally, to the Lord Jesus.
I say thanks for having mercy on me
and putting me in the ministry.

ACKNOWLEDGMENTS

My thanks and gratitude go to the following:
My siblings—I thank you all. Maame, thanks for your spiritual input, and Panyin, my twin brother, thanks for the editing and the encouragement.

My staff—Amps-Bee, thank you for standing with me. Anita, you are great. Victoria, thank you for your great help in writing this book. Mary C, thanks for your input.

All pastors and members of LCI Apaché and LCI Morning Star Cathedral—I cannot forget you. I love you for your support and care.

CONTENTS

    Foreword by Bishop Dag Heward-Mills xi
1. Living With the Enemy 1
2. Physical Squatters 9
3. Spiritual Squatters 17
4. The History of Demons 29
5. The Abode of Demons 33
6. Can a Spirit Inhabit a House? 43
7. Let God Arise 49
8. Let Us Pray 59
9. Rest on Every Side 63
10. Hosting the Holy Spirit 71
    About Kakra Baiden 79
    Contact the Author 81

FOREWORD

PROPHET KAKRA BAIDEN brings more than twenty years of experience to bear in this powerful book that he has titled *Squatters*. I deem it a privilege to be asked to write the foreword for his very first book. Having established churches and built large congregations, Kakra Baiden has distinguished himself in the ministry as a faithful pastor and teacher.

Also, as the years have gone by, Kakra has gradually metamorphosed into a distinctive prophet with the gifts of "seeing" and "knowing" being manifested regularly in his ministry. I myself have been enchanted and awed with his fantastic testimonies of journeys into the supernatural world of spirits, where the events and happenings of our lives are determined. I recognize a genuine and anointed prophetic stream in Kakra Baiden that has only just begun to flow as a mighty river, and I always look forward to more prophetic revelations from him.

This book will enlighten you by revealing the realities of

the spirit world that lie beyond the veil. It will encourage you to be spiritual and to trust in God rather than in the arm of flesh. I also believe that this book in your hand will be a channel of blessing and healing every time you read it. I highly recommend this book, *Squatters*, to you.

May you be set free from the powers of darkness through the anointing and revelation within these pages.

—Bishop Dag Heward-Mills

CHAPTER 1

LIVING WITH THE ENEMY

Now as Jannes and Jambres withstood Moses, so do these also resist the truth: men of corrupt minds, reprobate concerning the faith.

—2 Timothy 3:8

I REMEMBER THE DAY clearly. It was a Tuesday night service, and I had just finished delivering a sermon in church. Suddenly I heard the Holy Spirit whisper in my ear, "Can you see that woman in the red dress sitting on your left-hand side, about four rows away?" I looked toward that direction and saw her. "Call her and pray for her," He said.

After hesitating for a few seconds, I pointed in her direction and said, "That woman over there, come to me." With a puzzled expression on her face, she rose up and walked gingerly toward me. She was in her middle twenties, slim, chocolate-colored, and about five and a half feet tall.

As she walked toward me, I heard the Holy Spirit say again to me, "Pray for her and release the spirit of prayer and supplication." I knew enough of the Scriptures to know that this was a quotation from Zechariah 12:10, "And I will pour upon the house of David, and upon the inhabitants of Jerusalem, the spirit of grace and of supplications: and they shall look upon me whom they have pierced..." Immediately I knew the Lord wanted me to pray so that the grace for prayer would be released.

This was not new to me, because the Holy Spirit had once instructed me in a meeting to lay hands on a certain woman for the same grace. She came back later to tell me how she had prayed continuously for three days and could not even go to work.

In this regard, I obeyed the Holy Spirit and laid hands on her and prayed, releasing the grace for prayer. I kept wondering why the Lord asked me to pray for this particular woman. But two days after this incident I came to understand how important that prayer was.

This is her story of what happened that fateful Tuesday night after the service.

Snake in the Bedroom

She told me:

> After the meeting I went home and retired to bed. As soon as I fell on my bed, the Holy Spirit took control of my tongue, and prayer started pouring out from my innermost being. I could not stop myself. Two hours passed, and I continued to travail in prayer. The night wore on, and I started feeling sleepy. I closed my eyes momentarily, and suddenly I saw you [Prophet Baiden] in a vision. "Do not sleep, pray," you said to me. I was startled, and immediately I felt reenergized and continued praying.

It was then I heard a loud screeching noise like the sound of some sort of machine in my room. Since there was a sawmill close to my house, I assumed the sound was coming from there, so I dismissed it and continued earnestly in prayer. This screeching noise continued throughout the night. But it did not scare me; I kept on praying till morning. Truly, the grace for prayer had been released upon me. This was completely unusual for me. It was a supernatural experience!

In the morning I got ready and set off for work. As I sat on the bus, I felt something like a volcano start up within me, and it wasn't long before I started bubbling with prayer. With that kind of feeling, I was certain I could not go to work. I decided to go home and continue in prayer.

As soon as I got to my bedroom, I lay on the bed and started praying again.

Unexpectedly I heard a loud screeching noise that sounded like the one I had been hearing the whole night.

As I cast an anxious look round my room, the most amazing thing happened. I saw my wardrobe open, and this huge snake, with steely beady eyes, stuck out its enormous head. It made a loud screeching noise. I opened my mouth in disbelief; my heart froze, my hair stood up, goose pimples came all over me, and my heart begun to beat faster than normal. Then adrenaline took over. I jumped out of the bed and raced out of the room with the screeching noise trailing after me. With a loud bang I shut the door behind me and started screaming for help.

Naturally my brother stepped out of his room into the corridor to find out what the commotion was all about. He took one look at my frightened face and immediately knew something had gone terribly wrong. "What is wrong?" he shouted. I replied with a quavering voice, "Sn-a-k-e, there is a s-n-a-ke in my room."

Subsequently we made our way to the door, and he opened it slightly to peek. There it was; this huge, long, black snake relaxing on my bed. My brother armed himself with a big wooden club and entered the room. The snake moved from the bed and went to hide behind the wardrobe. I saw the snake coming from his blind side preparing to strike.

I shouted hysterically, "It is behind you." Instinctively he swung the wooden club and caught the snake by the head, smashing it at the edge of the bed. What a relief that was!

Later on I begun to reflect on the events of the previous night and realized that the Lord had saved me. Little did I know that my prayer would keep the snake locked in the wardrobe throughout the night. Indeed, an invisible force kept it locked inside the wardrobe. The reason why I needed to pray was that God knew the danger that awaited me. Had I not prayed, I would have died from a snake bite.

What a story! You may be sceptical about this story as you read. You may wonder, "Is this a fairy tale?" This is a story coming from the horse's own mouth. What else do you want to believe?

In 2 Timothy 3:8 Paul, writing to Timothy, commented on spiritual conditions in the last days: "As Jannes and Jambres withstood Moses, so do these also resist the truth." Jannes and Jambres were the two magicians who opposed Moses.

If you know the story very well, you remember they

threw down their sticks and turned them into snakes. From this scripture we learn one feature of the last days: Satan and his agents will manifest physically, and the climax of this will be the manifestation of the antichrist—a satanic agent in human form.

Second Thessalonians 2:8–9 states, "And then shall that Wicked be revealed, whom the Lord shall consume with the spirit of his mouth, and shall destroy with the brightness of his coming: Even him, whose coming is after the working of Satan with all power and signs and lying wonders."

Satan can manifest himself tangibly just like the Holy Spirit. That snake was a physical manifestation of a satanic presence. There was a demonic presence in her room, and it took spiritual warfare to control the situation.

Demons in the Bedroom

One day I heard a knock at the front door of the flat where I used to live with my wife and kids. When I opened the door, a young man in his late teens stood in the doorway. I smiled as I welcomed him. He was one of the dynamic, zealous brothers in our church. My smile beat a hasty retreat when I saw the worried look on his face. I ushered him quickly into a chair and asked him what the problem was.

With his voice laced with grief, he croaked, "Pastor, it's my dad. He needs help."

I asked anxiously, "What is wrong with him?"

"He is under severe spiritual attack. There are evil spirits terrorizing him to the extent that he cannot sleep. Can you please go with me to see him? He needs help." Seeing how troubled he was, I asked him to take the lead to his father's house and promised to follow.

Within an hour I was at the house. A man, probably in his sixties, was at the door to receive me. He had worry painted all over his face.

I entered the living room, and we sat down to talk. I could see tears welling up in his eyes as he began to talk. One could tell the pain he was going through.

He said, "Pastor, something terrible is happening in this house. For three days now I have not been able to sleep." With the tears now flowing more freely, he continued, "Each time I try to sleep, I see two beings charging toward me to claim my soul. I know that if I close my eyes, they will claim my soul and I will not live again."

He brushed aside his tears and continued. "I have been awake for the past three days, and I am suffering."

As I listened to the story, a gist of the solution began to form in my spirit. I said to him, "I think I know who these beings are."

Anxiously he asked, "Who are they?" I replied, "I suspect you are being harassed by two evil spirits: *hell* and *death*."

Scripture states clearly that death is a spirit being and hell is not only a place but also a spirit being. When an unsaved person dies, the spirit of death comes to claim the spirit of the person. He is the spirit that claims the soul of those who are spiritually dead or alienated from the life of God. Death hands over his captive to the spirit of hell, who is his partner. Hell then escorts the person to the place called hell.

DEATH AND HELL

In Revelation 6:8 the Bible sheds light on the *modus operandi* of this gang. This is how John describes their operation:

"And I looked, and behold a pale horse: and his name that sat on him was Death, and Hell followed with him. And power was given unto them over the fourth part of the earth, to kill with sword, and with hunger, and with death, and with the beasts of the earth."

When a Christian dies, he does not meet these two spirits. The Lord Jesus ushers him into heaven.

That is why Jesus said in John 8:51, "If a man keep my saying, he shall never see death." He was not talking about physical death. He was talking about the spiritual being called death. May you escape hell and death in Jesus's name. Amen!

When Stephen was being stoned to death, he said, "Behold, I see the heavens opened, and the Son of man standing at the right hand of God" (Acts 7:56). Then he cried and said in verse 59, "Lord Jesus, receive my spirit." He went straight to heaven. This is the lot of the believer.

This is pretty clear to me because I had a near-death experience once as an unbeliever, and the spirit of death came for my soul. It was the mercy of God that offered me another chance to come back to life.

I knew that the man was being threatened by death and hell. After inquiries, I found out that he was not born again. I told him the first thing he had to do was to give his life to Christ. He agreed instantly. We shared a prayer, and I led him to Christ.

I then asked him to show me where he had been seeing these beings so I could pray and dismiss these *spiritual squatters* (as I call them) from his house. He pointed toward his bedroom door and said, "When I am about to sleep, I see them standing here." We made our way into his bedroom, and I spread my hands to the Lord and began to command any spirit that inhabited his room to leave.

After that prayer I said to him, "From today on, you will sleep like a baby because 'He gives His beloved sleep.' The enemies you have seen today, you will see them again no more."

The following morning I dropped by to see how he was doing, and this time, when he opened the door, a wide smile filled his face. He said, "Pastor, the demons are gone. I slept like a baby as you said."

Both the young woman and the sixty-year-old man had to contend with demonic spiritual squatters in their homes.

In the next chapters I will be shedding light on spiritual squatters and how you can eject them completely from your life and maintain the presence of God in your life.

CHAPTER 2

PHYSICAL SQUATTERS

> *But if ye will not drive out the inhabitants of the land from before you; then it shall come to pass, that those which ye let remain of them shall be pricks in your eyes, and thorns in your sides, and shall vex you in the land wherein ye dwell.*
>
> —Numbers 33:55

THE WORD *SQUATTER* means someone who settles on a land without a valid title, lease, or monthly tenancy. A squatter gains legal title by what is termed in legal parlance as "adverse possession." If the squatter adversely possesses the land for a considerable period of time, the law deems him to be the owner and his title trumps that of the original legal owner.

Santana

I remember when I was growing up as a young boy, there was a mentally deranged man who used to live in an abandoned building that used to house an electrical transformer.

His name was Santana. This building was in front of my friend Charles's house. Since Santana was deranged, the idea of him living close to Charles's house worried him a lot. So we hatched a plan to burn all his belongings in a bid to get him to move out of the place.

A fine opportunity came up one day, and we burnt his belongings. The next morning when Charles woke up, he discovered to his dismay that Santana had moved into their garage with the few belongings he had left. He had neither the right, title, or lease in order for him to live there. He was now a squatter in their house.

A Land That I Will Show You

Most of the conflicts in this world are over land and its resources. At the root of the wars in the Middle East is the land question, and this root expresses itself in the branches of terrorism, war, bloodshed, and conflict. The biblical history of the land of Israel can be traced to Abraham.

> Now the Lord had said unto Abram, Get thee out of thy country, and from thy kindred, and from thy father's house, unto a land that I will shew thee.
> —Genesis 12:1

Abraham and his seed were supposed to inherit this land forever. He finally possessed the land when his father died and Lot his nephew departed from him.

> And the Lord said unto Abram, after that Lot was separated from him, Lift up now thine eyes, and look from the place where thou art northward, and southward, and eastward, and westward: For all the

land which thou seest, to thee will I give it, and to
thy seed for ever.
—Genesis 13:14–15

There are people who will prevent you from entering your God-given inheritance until you part company with them. Eventually famine sent Abraham's descendants out of the land into Egypt in Joseph's time. They abandoned the land and created a vacuum. In no time, there arose a new king over Egypt who did not know Joseph. They had overstayed their welcome and so were turned into slaves. But God sent Moses to deliver them and bring them back to their inheritance. The only problem at this time was that the land was no longer free. It was now occupied by squatters.

Squatters Occupy the Land of Israel

And the Lord said, I have surely seen the affliction of my people which are in Egypt, and have heard their cry by reason of their taskmasters; for I know their sorrows; and I am come down to deliver them out of the hand of the Egyptians, and to bring them up out of that land unto a good land and a large, unto a land flowing with milk and honey; unto the place of the Canaanites, and the Hittites, and the Amorites, and the Perizzites, and the Hivites, and the Jebusites.
—Exodus 3:7–8

The squatters who came to occupy the land during this fallow period were the Canaanites, Hittites, Amorites, Perizzites, and Jebusites.

There is a cliché that says, "Nature abhors a vacuum." This shows how dangerous it is to leave a vacuum in your life. If you leave your marital home, someone else may take over your marital duties. If you fail to live with your children, Satan may take that responsibility and raise them up. If you have a lot of idle time, Satan may find a job for you to do. If you leave yourself spiritually empty, an evil spirit may move in.

Do not leave any vacuum in your life. Make sure every area of your life is filled with the principles of the word and the presence of the Lord.

I have had an unpleasant experience of dealing with squatters.

THE SNAKE AND THE CURSE

When we bought the building for the first church I pastored, I remember it was an old warehouse that had been deserted for many years. After we had paid for the land and concluded the whole deal, we realized we had a new battle on our hands. The *squatters* who occupied the site were unwilling to move. It was both a physical and spiritual battle.

Physically we had to force them to leave the land. Spiritually we had to pray continually. On the day they left, the leader of the squatters removed a god that he had buried in the ground; it was the head of a snake. He raised it up, looked me in the eye, muttered some incantations, and cursed me. I refuted it in Jesus's name.

Multiple land ownership will always be a flashpoint of conflict. It is amazing how people fight for things they have no right or title to. The land was ours, but we had squatters contesting over its ownership.

This was the warning God gave to His people on their way to possess Canaan, their Promised Land.

> But if ye will not drive out the inhabitants of the land from before you; then it shall come to pass, that those which ye let remain of them shall be *pricks* in your eyes, and *thorns* in your sides, and shall vex you in the land wherein ye dwell.
> —NUMBERS 33:55, EMPHASIS ADDED

The fight for the land was not just natural but also spiritual. These people did not just exercise a physical presence. They also exercised a spiritual one.

PHYSICAL SQUATTERS ARE PRICKS AND THORNS

When you buy a land that has multiple owners, you will experience pricks (a stinging pain), thorns (irritation and annoyance), and vexation (disturbance of the peace of mind). If you have squatters on your land, they will cause you pain and irritation, and they will disturb your peace of mind. Let me ask you a question. Have you ever bought a piece of land with multiple owners? Well, I have, and believe me, it is not a pleasant experience.

Somebody once gave me money to purchase a parcel of land. After buying the land, we decided to secure the plot. We walled it off and dumped building materials on it. Knowing how secured the plot was, we did not visit the site for about two years. After a while, we visited the site, and to our shock, someone had built a beautiful house on the plot with our building materials. You can imagine what ensued afterward. It brought pain, irritation, and disturbance since we had to fight legal battles with its resultant financial costs.

For Israel to have peace, God advised them to eject every squatter from the land. Being passive will not help when you are dealing with squatters. You have to stand and fight. I urge you now to do the same, in Jesus's name. Amen!

War and Peace

Sometimes to have peace, you must make war. David was able to hand over a peaceful kingdom to his son Solomon because he had fought and subdued every single squatter. This was what Solomon said about his father in 1 Kings 5:3–4.

> Thou knowest how that David my father could not build an house unto the name of the Lord his God for the wars which were about him on every side, until the Lord put them under the soles of his feet. But now the Lord my God hath given me rest on every side, so that there is neither adversary nor evil occurrent.
> —1 Kings 5:3–4

Ecclesiastes 3:8 says there is "a time to love, and a time to hate; *a time of war, and a time of peace*" (emphasis added). Sometimes war will have to precede peace for peace to be established. Psalm 29:11 says, "The Lord will give strength unto his people; the Lord will bless his people with peace." This means that God will give strength to His people to fight, and the result of this fight will be peace.

There are some Christians who are pacifists in many situations, but there are situations that call for war. When you buy land with multiple owners, you may have to fight back.

When another woman is trying to take your husband from you, fight back. Do not cower into a hasty retreat, as was the case of a woman who called me one day to tell me she wanted to leave her home because someone was trying to take her husband away from her. I told her to stay and fight!

WARS YOU MUST FIGHT

When the devil is fighting to steal your health, fight him back. Do not listen to the negative doctor's report; listen to God, for you shall not die but live to declare the works of the Lord.

When you are interested in someone, do not let another person scare you away with his luxurious car. Fight and win the love of your life. David killed his Goliath in order to bring peace to Israel. You must dare to kill yours. Amen!

The time has come for us to stand up for what we believe. We must fight until we are victorious. The apostle Paul encourages us to fight the good fight of faith.

It is a good fight, because the result has already been predetermined; we are winners! All we need to do is to stay on our feet until the final bell.

The squatter in your life must leave NOW!

CHAPTER 3

SPIRITUAL SQUATTERS

*While we look not at the things which are
seen, but at the things which are not seen: for
the things which are seen are temporal; but
the things which are not seen are eternal.*

—2 Corinthians 4:18

WHAT IS TRUE of land ownership in the physical realm is even truer in the spiritual realm. Just as there are physical owners of a land, there are spiritual owners. The fact that you have physical ownership of a place with a title deed does not make you a spiritual owner. That is why it is possible to be a physical owner of a land or property and not be a spiritual owner. I wonder who the spiritual owner of your land is.

If it is an evil spirit, it means that it has become a squatter on your land, which will eventually become a prick in your eyes and a thorn in your sides.

"How can this be true?" you ask.

Well, I know this for a fact because Scripture and experience has taught me so.

The Spirit of Death

I remember the second time Jesus appeared to me; I was in the university at that time. I had just returned from an early morning prayer meeting and was sitting on my bed singing softly to myself. I heard a firm but gentle knock on the door. I answered, "Come in."

The door opened and Jesus came in. I stood up and muttered in utter disbelief, "Jesus," and He smiled in return. He told me there was something He wanted me to do. I asked Him what it was, and He said, "I want you to fast and pray. I want you to intercede on behalf of this hall of residence."

I inquired, "What for?"

"Do you know why people are dying in this hall?" He asked.

I replied "No!"

At that time people were dying in the hall for various reasons. An example was a case of one gentleman who committed suicide. That was how bad the situation was.

Up until that time I never assigned any spiritual reason to these deaths. It was then I understood the scripture that said, "For though we walk in the flesh, we do not war after the flesh" (2 Cor. 10:3).

"The reason why people are dying in this hall is because the spirit of death has occupied the hall. That is why I want you to fast and pray for three days in order to drive out this spirit," He continued. I obeyed and went ahead to fast and pray. After doing this successfully, death ceased in the hall. There was no report of death in the hall until I completed the university.

THE WOMAN IN A COMA

In another incident I visited a woman in the hospital who was in coma. I went there with her parents and other family members. In that particular ward there were three other women who were conscious and appeared strong. As I began to pray, I suddenly discerned the presence of the spirit of death standing at her bedside. I rebuked the spirit to leave the woman alone. Her parents were not happy with me after this because apparently they did not believe in such prayers.

The following day I went to the hospital, only to learn that the three women who appeared strong and healthy had died during the night. On the other hand, the woman who had fallen into coma was still alive and kicking. She later recovered and was discharged from the hospital.

Consequently I realized how important that prayer was. It saved her life. It is possible the spirit of death attacked the other women due to frustration.

To understand this scripturally and clearly, it will be prudent to be familiar with the history of land ownership in the Bible.

THE HISTORY OF LAND OWNERSHIP

> And God said, Let us make man in our image, after our likeness: and let them have dominion over the fish of the sea, and over the fowl of the air, and over the cattle, and over all the earth, and over every creeping thing that creepeth upon the earth.
> —GENESIS 1:26

According to Genesis chapter 1, God created the world, including the sea and land, and when Adam was ready to marry, God gave it to him as a wedding present. God gave Adam dominion over all the earth.

The word *dominion* can be defined as a territorial possession controlled by a ruling state. In this instance the state was Adam, and he controlled the whole earth, both physically and spiritually. This means that he combined physical ownership with spiritual ownership. In the course of time, however, Satan tempted Adam and Eve and made them eat the forbidden fruit. Eventually God drove them out of the Garden of Eden.

PHYSICAL AND SPIRITUAL CONTROL

The first recorded implication in Scripture was that they came under a curse. It is worthy to note that there are other implications that are not recorded in Genesis but elsewhere in the Scriptures. One implication was the fact that they lost spiritual control of the land but retained the physical control. This distinction is very crucial. Land ownership, therefore, was split into two sections: spiritual and physical ownership.

Physical control went to Adam and Eve. They farmed and built on the land. This control still rests in the hands of the Adamic race. Spiritual control of the land, nonetheless, went into the hands of Satan, and since then the devil has become the god of this world.

This is how Paul described the devil: "...the god of this world hath blinded the minds of them which believe not" (2 Cor. 4:4).

THE TEMPTATION OF JESUS

The temptation of Jesus in Luke 4 sheds greater light on this subject.

> And the devil, taking him up into an high mountain, shewed unto him all the kingdoms of the world in

> a moment of time. And the devil said unto him, All this power will I give thee, and the glory of them: for that is delivered unto me; and to whomsoever I will I give it. If thou therefore wilt worship me, all shall be thine. And Jesus answered and said unto him, Get thee behind me, Satan: for it is written, Thou shalt worship the Lord thy God, and him only shalt thou serve.
> —LUKE 4:5–8

The devil showed Jesus all the nations of the world and offered the glory of it. A country's glory is its infrastructure and finances—buildings, roads, and so forth. He showed him America, Europe, Africa, Asia, and Australia. He offered him the real estate, showed him the parcels of land, and said, "All this is given unto me."

But what he offered was occupied physically by the Romans. In fact, the scribes had their houses on it. Jesus Himself had His home there. Pilate also had built his house on it. So clearly the land had physical owners, and therefore in order for one to own a plot of land, one did not have to purchase the title deed from the devil.

What Satan was offering was not physical control but spiritual control of the lands. If it were not true that Satan had that level of control, it would not have been a temptation at all.

The word *delivered* is the Greek word *paradidomi*. It is the same word that is translated as "betrayed" when referring to Judas Iscariot. He betrayed Jesus in Matthew 10:5. In other words, Satan said Adam betrayed God and handed over these kingdoms to him. Satan and his agents control all the lands spiritually.

Jesus said concerning the devil in John 14:30, "…the prince of this world cometh, and hath nothing in me." The word *prince* is the Greek word that means, "chief ruler, first in rank, or power." In other words, Satan is the chief ruler of the world.

In Ephesians 2:2, this is how Paul described them before their conversion with Christ. "Wherein in times past ye walked according to the course of this world, according to the prince of the power of the air, the spirit that now worketh in the children of disobedience."

He told Christians in Ephesus that before they came to the Lord, they were under the influence of the devil.

One thing worth noting is the realm in which Satan rules. Paul says he rules the air or the spirit realm, meaning his control is spiritual.

The "Four-Hundred-Year" Squatter

When I moved into my own house, I had a very interesting vision that I want to share with you.

Because I am a prophet, I can be in two worlds at the same time. I can be physically asleep and spiritually awake. Sometimes it becomes difficult to tell whether I am awake or asleep. I empathize with Paul when he said, "I knew a man in Christ above fourteen years ago, (whether in the body, I cannot tell; or whether out of the body, I cannot tell...)" (2 Cor. 12:2).

I saw my spirit wake up in the middle of the night and walk to the driveway. As I stood there, I saw a little shack erected on my lawn. I was very puzzled and drew closer to inspect the structure.

I realized it was someone's little house. I said to myself, "How come I have not seen this house before?" In anger I approached the shack and banged on the door. A head poked out of the door and a short man emerged. I confronted him,

"What are you doing on my plot?" He seemed equally surprised and said to me, "I am the spirit that lives on this land. I have been living here for the past four hundred years, and you are rather trespassing." In fury I commanded him to leave my property in the name of Jesus. He quickly dismantled his shack and moved out of my land. This was a demonic power who was contesting the ownership of the land with me spiritually. I had to wrestle him out of the place.

THE KINGDOM OF SATAN

> For we wrestle not against flesh and blood, but against principalities, against powers, against the rulers of the darkness of this world, against spiritual wickedness in high places.
> —EPHESIANS 6:12

Satan's kingdom has different levels of power and authority. When Satan took control of the land, he assigned evil spirits to be in charge. The first in rank are the *principalities*. The word *principality* means "principal, the first or chief." It was one such spirit that ruled over the kingdom of Persia in Daniel's day. An angel said to Daniel, "But the prince of the kingdom of Persia withstood me one and twenty days" (Dan. 10:13). There was a principality ruling over that land.

Next in rank are the *powers*. The word *power* in Greek means, "a delegated influence with jurisdiction." There are also *the rulers of the darkness of this world*. These, I believe, are the land guards who spiritually control lands on behalf of their master. I suppose it was such a spirit I came into contact with.

SPIRITUAL SQUATTERS ARE PRICKS AND THORNS

My father's experience

Inasmuch as *squatters* were pricks and thorns to Israel, *spiritual squatters* become pricks and thorns to us when we cohabit with them.

Some years ago my father fell ill. He went to a number of hospitals and saw several doctors, but no one could tell the cause of the disease. At one point he became bedridden. We all feared he was going to die since no one could fathom what was wrong with him.

One day a prayer team from his church came to his bedroom to pray with him for healing. They prayed for about one hour. Nothing happened to him while the prayer was going on; he was still sick. According to him, that same night as he slept, he was abruptly awoken around 2:00 a.m., and suddenly a very bright light engulfed the whole room. (Do you remember Paul's vision on the road to Damascus? He saw a supernatural light.) I believe it was a similar experience.

At this point my father realized he was not alone in the room. Standing at his bedside were two women and one little boy. They seemed startled because the light had come on unexpectedly. Realizing they had been exposed, they covered their faces and fled out of his room. The bright lights then began to recede, and the room became dark again. Instantly he knew he had received a visitation from the Lord.

> And the light shineth in darkness; and the darkness comprehended it not.
> —JOHN 1:5

When the glory of God shines in the spirit realm, the power of darkness cannot withstand it.

He suddenly felt healed and strong. He tried to get out of his bed and realized he could do so with ease. He decided to walk downstairs for the first time in many weeks, and he did so easily. God had healed him completely! He started rejoicing in Jesus. He woke my mother up and told her he had been healed. Initially my mother did not believe it, but she later realized that truly God had healed him.

What I want you to observe in this story is that those three spiritual beings (the women and little boy) were the cause of his sickness. The minute they were ejected from his room, he was healed instantly. Could there be a squatter in your room?

THE PESTILENCE THAT WALKS IN DARKNESS

One of the things that God protects us from is the pestilence that walks in darkness. Psalm 91 talks about the protection of God. Verse 6 makes reference to a spirit being.

> Thou shalt not be afraid for the terror by night; nor for the arrow that flieth by day; nor for the pestilence that *walketh* in darkness; nor for the destruction that wasteth at noonday.
> —PSALM 91:5–6, EMPHASIS ADDED

The word *pestilence* means an epidemic disease with a high death rate. This kind of disease can be administered by demonic affliction because it is a pestilence that walks. Do not forget; the demons that dwell on land walk about.

In Luke 11:24 Jesus said, "When the unclean spirit is gone out of a man, he walketh through dry places..."

Spirits can come into a house and afflict the occupants

with deadly diseases without necessarily possessing them. The assignment of these spirit beings is to afflict people with diseases. They mostly operate at night. Though there are diseases that have physical causes, I believe there are some that are caused by demons.

In Matthew 8:16 Scripture records the healing ministry of Jesus: "When the even was come, they brought unto him many that were possessed with devils: and he cast out the *spirits* with his word, and healed all that were sick" (emphasis added).

The people Jesus healed were sick because of demonic oppression. That is why they received their healing after the spirits had been cast out.

THE DEMON OF HYPERTENSION

In the Book of Job the devil, a spirit being, went to Job's house and afflicted him with a disease. This is how the Bible describes it:

> So went Satan forth from the presence of the Lord, and smote Job with sore boils from the sole of his foot unto his crown.
> —JOB 2:7

One day I was asleep in my room when I saw a demon making its way from the gate to my room. I watched as this small shadowy figure made its way through my gate. It came through the front door, through the corridor, and then entered my room. He jumped on my chest and opened my pajama buttons. He cut the area above my heart and took out something from its pocket.

Just as he was about to insert it into my heart, I screamed at it, "I bind you in the name of Jesus!" It jumped off my chest and ran out of the house. I knew it wanted to afflict me with the disease of hypertension. What it did not know, however, was that I was spiritually awake while this was going on.

You may have your doubts and say this is impossible. I believe it is perfectly scriptural.

Rent This House, Please!

One day I went to pray for a man who had difficulty renting out his house. I went to the house to pray for God to grant him favor for the house to be rented. For me it was the usual routine—a pastoral assignment—so I thought little of it. I prayed a general prayer and went back home.

That night I had a vision. In this vision I had gone back to the house. Paul said in 1 Corinthians 5:3 that he was absent in body but present in spirit. It is therefore possible for one's spirit to be present in a place where one's body is not.

I started moving from room to room. Every room I entered was empty, until I opened a door to a particular room. In this room sat this spirit that looked like a woman made out of transparent glass. As soon as she saw me, she raised her hand and started chanting. I burst into tongues, and before long, she was out of the house. God drove her out of the house.

Subsequently the Lord instructed me to return to the house with anointing oil and pray over the place. I went back to the house the following day and did as God instructed. I prayed that every squatter would be ejected by the spirit of God.

Do you know what happened? That very afternoon the house was rented. The spiritual squatter who was preventing the house from being rented out had been ejected.

CHAPTER 4

THE HISTORY OF DEMONS

For we wrestle not against flesh and blood, but against principalities, against powers, against the rulers of the darkness of this world, against spiritual wickedness in high places.

—Ephesians 6:12

In 1 Corinthians 13:9 the Bible states that we prophesy in part. "For we know in part, and we prophesy in part." This means that prophecy only gives us a glimpse of a picture, not the whole thing.

The Book of Job is one of my favorite books in the Bible. This is because it teaches a lot about spiritual warfare.

> Take, my brethren, the prophets, who have spoken in the name of the Lord, for an example of suffering affliction and of patience.... Ye have heard of the patience of Job...
>
> —James 5:10–11

Squatters

According to James, Job was a prophet. If you are familiar with the story, you will recall that Job was a wealthy, holy, and prosperous man whom the Lord had blessed and was pleased with.

Upon permission from God, Satan attacked him. He destroyed his finances, ruined his business, killed his children, and disturbed his harmonious marriage through many natural occurrences. These were carried out by demons.

In this entire story Job was unaware that all the attacks, although natural, were caused by satanic activity. Through the lens of Scripture we have the privilege of knowing who it was that attacked him.

In chapter 30 Job had begun to prophesy about the identity of his enemies. I would like us to examine a portion of this scripture where he prophesies about the origin and activities of these enemies.

> They were driven forth from among men, (they cried after them as after a thief;) to dwell in the cliffs of the valleys, in caves of the earth, and in the rocks. Among the bushes they brayed; under the nettles they were gathered together. They were children of fools, yea, children of base men: they were viler than the earth. And now am I their song, yea, I am their byword. They abhor me, they flee far from me, and spare not to spit in my face. Because he hath loosed my cord, and afflicted me, they have also let loose the bridle before me. Upon my right hand rise the youth; they push away my feet, and they raise up against me the ways of their destruction.
> —Job 30:5–12

From the preceding verses we gather certain facts about demons. Our enemies seem to be disembodied spirits who once lived on the earth but were banished from living among men. When they were disembodied, they inhabited trees, plants, rocks, and caves.

I want you to notice that they can inhabit caves, which are like rooms.

For me, this explains why lesser gods can be found in rivers, stones, bushes, and rocks. I believe these are demons inhabiting inanimate things.

CHAPTER 5

THE ABODE OF DEMONS

> *When the unclean spirit is gone out of a man, he walketh through dry places, seeking rest; and finding none, he saith, I will return unto my house whence I came out.*
>
> —Luke 11:24

Life is shaped by two forces—spiritual and natural. These forces ultimately decide our destiny. Ignorance in any form is dangerous, be it mental or spiritual. There are many educated people who are spiritual illiterates.

The Dangers of Ignorance

Isaiah 5:13 reminds us of the dangers of spiritual illiteracy. "Therefore my people are gone into captivity, because they have no knowledge: and their honourable men are famished, and their multitude dried up with thirst." God said, "They are My people all right but it does not make them immune from the effects of ignorance."

One result of ignorance is captivity; you become enslaved by what you do not know. Hosea 4:6 says the same thing: "My people are destroyed for lack of knowledge…" What you do not know can destroy you.

The story of Job talks about a hardworking righteous businessman whom God had blessed tremendously in every facet of life. One day his fortunes changed suddenly for the worse.

He lost his wealth, children, and health. The change in his fortunes was as a result of a change in his spiritual fortunes. God removed the walls of spiritual protection around him and gave the devil permission to attack him.

> And the Lord said unto Satan, Behold, all that he hath is in thy power; only upon himself put not forth thine hand. So Satan went forth from the presence of the Lord.
>
> —Job 1:12

In his spiritual ignorance Job attributed all his misfortune to God. He said, "…The Lord gave, and the Lord hath taken away; blessed be the name of the Lord" (Job 1:21). But ti was not the Lord who took away from him; it was the devil!

He did not know that "…we wrestle not against flesh and blood, but against principalities, against powers, against the rulers of the darkness of this world, against spiritual wickedness in high places" (Eph. 6:12).

He did not know that "…though we walk in the flesh, we do not war after the flesh" (2 Cor. 10:3).

He interpreted everything from a natural point of view. This led to his captivity and destruction.

What was Job ignorant about?

Job was ignorant of the fact that evil spirits have the capacity to live and inhabit different environments.

THE DWELLING PLACES OF DEMONS

What are the dwelling places of demons? I believe there are several.

In Luke 11 Jesus healed a man who was dumb by casting out the evil spirit that was afflicting him. After that, He proceeded to teach about the activities of demons. There are certain things He said that are noteworthy.

> When the unclean spirit is gone out of a man, he walketh through dry places, seeking rest; and finding none, he saith, I will return unto my house whence I came out. And when he cometh, he findeth it swept and garnished. Then goeth he, and taketh to him seven other spirits more wicked than himself; and they enter in, and dwell there: and the last state of that man is worse than the first.
> —LUKE 11:24–26

THE FAVORITE HOTEL OF AN EVIL SPIRIT IS THE HUMAN BODY!

When the evil spirit departed, Jesus made a comment on the habitation of demons. He said, "When the unclean spirit is gone out of a man, he walketh through dry places, seeking rest; and finding none, he saith, I will return unto my house whence I came out" (Luke 11:24).

The Bible says the demon was seeking rest. The literal translation for this is "recreation."

I want you to notice; the evil spirit referred to the man's body as "my house." His body was his accommodation.

I once cast out a deaf spirit from the body of a man.

After prayer the spirit came out with a loud shriek, and immediately the man's hearing was restored!

The first choice place of residence for demons is the human body. To them, the human body represents a five-star hotel where they have the opportunity to express their personality because they are disembodied spirits.

Demons Have the Capacity to Inhabit Animals

Demons can reside in animals. I believe there are animals that are demonized. I once had an extremely vicious dog that I believe was demonized. I was forced to put it to sleep.

The demons in Mark 5 first inhabited the pigs before eventually going to dwell in the sea.

> Now there was there nigh unto the mountains a great herd of swine feeding. And all the devils besought him, saying, Send us into the swine, that we may enter into them.
> —Mark 5:11–12

Demons Have the Capacity to Inhabit Water

In Revelation 13:1 John had a vision and saw a spirit rise from the sea: "And I stood upon the sand of the sea, and saw a beast rise up out of the sea, having seven heads and ten horns, and upon his horns ten crowns, and upon his heads the name of blasphemy."

It is interesting to note the spirit John saw was dwelling in the sea. This point is buttressed by another scripture in Revelation. In Revelation 9:14 God said, "Loose the four angels which are bound in the great river Euphrates."

Angels are spirits, and in this instance there were four wicked spirits being held in the river Euphrates.

THE SPIRIT OF MADNESS

I suspect that one of the activities of spirits that come from the sea is schizophrenia or madness.

I was once praying for someone with that condition. For about two hours we prayed with little success. During the course of the prayer I fell into a trance. All my natural senses were suspended. I found myself underwater and saw the evil spirits who were afflicting this woman; they came from under the sea. I rebuked them and commanded them to let her go. The woman who was suffering from madness was healed instantly after this revelation.

The reason why I say this is because, in the account of the healing of the mad man of Gadara in Mark 5, the spirits who were afflicting him finally went into the sea.

> And forthwith Jesus gave them leave. And the unclean spirits went out, and entered into the swine: and the herd ran violently down a steep place into the sea, (they were about two thousand;) and were choked in the sea.
> —MARK 5:13

DEMONS HAVE THE CAPACITY TO LIVE UNDERGROUND

Demons also have the ability to live underground. Someone may say, "How?"

You see, in Revelation 13:11, John said, "And I beheld another beast coming up out of the earth; and he had two horns like a lamb, and he spake as a dragon."

This spirit came from underground.

I want to share with you a letter someone wrote to me concerning this:

"Spirits Vanish After I Poured the Anointing Oil"

Hello Prophet,
I attended the "Prophetic Celebration Convention" at the Qodesh, where you asked everyone to bring a bottle of anointing oil the following day for prayer. My wife was not at the Tuesday meeting, so I told her to get one for herself that Wednesday night.

After the service, we went home as usual in a very expectant mood, believing to do what we were asked to do. Everyone went to sleep, including my wife, so I decided to pray and anoint the rooms before going to bed. After 1:00 a.m. I retired to sleep.

When we woke up at dawn, my wife revealed to me a vision she had during her sleep. According to her, the middle (center) of our bedroom opened up and sunk in. In the depth of the ground were seated two old ladies by an old pot.

When my wife asked them what they were doing there, they replied that they had been on the land before her great-great-great-grandmother was born. They added that their main mission was to siphon people's finances into those pots. Prophet, I asked my wife whether she drove those ancestral spirits out in the vision, but she wasn't sure.

I picked my anointing oil in the morning and asked her to show me the exact location in the bedroom. I poured the oil at that particular spot.

I believe those spirits have been driven away in the name of our Lord Jesus Christ.

Prophet, may God bless you for the great work

you are doing, and may He continue to use you for the expansion of His kingdom. Amen!

The Lord opened the spiritual eye of this man's wife to show her the location of these spirits.

In the last days of King Saul he consulted a witch for guidance. This is part of the dialogue between Saul and the witch: "What sawest thou?" She answered and said, "I saw gods ascending out of the earth" (1 Sam. 28:13).

There were evil spirits resident underground, coming up out of the earth.

Demons Have the Capacity to Live on Land

The second observation I want you to make about demons is this: "When the unclean spirit is gone out of a man, he walketh through dry places…"

When the spirit left the man, it found alternative accommodation, and this time it was on a dry barren land.

> And when he cometh, he findeth it swept and garnished. Then goeth he, and taketh to him seven other spirits more wicked than himself; and they enter in, and dwell there: and the last state of that man is worse than the first.
> —Luke 11:25–26

On this land he found seven other evil spirits looking for a human body to occupy. This demon took them in as his roommates.

It is interesting to know that even in the demonic realms, there are accommodation problems.

I recently had a vision where a car had an accident.

Standing in the middle of the road was this demon that had caused the car to skid off the road and have an accident.

That is why it is important to pray when traveling because demons can live on land.

Demons Have the Capacity to Live in Buildings

The spirit living in a church

One day I visited a pastor friend of mine who was constructing his church building. After the evening service he showed me around the site. It was around 11:00 p.m. When we got to the fourth floor of their office block, I noticed a woman praying on the floor.

I asked my pastor friend why he had left this woman all alone in the middle of the night, when everyone had gone home. Apparently he was not seeing what I was seeing. I kept on insisting that there was a woman praying at the corner of the corridor. "I cannot see her," he replied.

Since there were no lights on that particular floor, I assumed it was the moonlight, which was not bright enough for him to see her. I pointed again toward the same direction, but he maintained there was no one there.

When I turned away from him to show him one more time, I noticed the woman had vanished. It dawned on me then that I was seeing into the spirit realm; God had opened my eyes to have vision.

The woman I saw was not a real woman but a spirit.

He also confirmed that others had seen visions concerning this spirit. They had even organized prayer and fasting times to drive the spirit out. He was amazed I had seen the spirit that resided in the church. It was a confirmation to him.

The Abode of Demons

The devil was unable to access Job's house because of three spiritual walls, or hedge, around him. These walls protected three things: first, him; second, his house; and third, all that he had.

> Hast not thou made an hedge about *him*, and about his *house*, and about *all* that he hath on every side? thou hast blessed the work of his hands, and his substance is increased in the land.
> —JOB 1:10, EMPHASIS ADDED

There is a major distinction in the Book of Job concerning demonic activity. God gave the devil access to Job's house and all that he had, but not Job himself.

The devil was restrained from touching him.

> And the Lord said unto Satan, Behold, all that he hath is in thy power; only upon himself put not forth thine hand. So Satan went forth from the presence of the Lord.
> —JOB 1:12

Job did not know that evil spirits have the capacity to inhabit buildings.

CHAPTER 6

CAN A SPIRIT INHABIT A HOUSE?

Know ye not that ye are the temple of God, and that the Spirit of God dwelleth in you?
—1 Corinthians 3:16

THE HOLY SPIRIT primarily lives in men. Nevertheless, He can also inhabit a building. A classic example is the events on the day of Pentecost.

> And when the day of Pentecost was fully come, they were all with one accord in one place. And suddenly there came a sound from heaven as of a rushing mighty wind, and it *filled all the house* where they were sitting. And there appeared unto them cloven tongues like as of fire, and it sat upon each of them. And they were all filled with the Holy Ghost, and began to speak with other tongues, as the Spirit gave them utterance.
> —Acts 2:1–4

It Filled the House

The Spirit of God filled the house first, and then He filled the people in the house. Note that those who were outside the house were not filled. This is because they were not present in the house.

If the Holy Spirit can fill a house, an evil spirit can also inhabit a house. This is because they are all spirits. I pray that the Holy Spirit will fill your house with His presence!

The account in Acts 2:1–4 is a typical example of the Holy Spirit filling both men and space. Sometimes during a service the manifested presence of God fills the room. What is of interest to me is the way the Spirit that filled the house influenced them. The Spirit influenced them to the extent that He affected their conduct, speech, and emotions. They began to speak in different tongues. They began to walk like drunken men. The Spirit influenced their behavior and emotions. They became bold as they preached the gospel.

From this we can infer that the presence of a particular spirit in a house can affect the speech, emotions, and conduct of the people in the house.

The Spirit of Divorce

I believe there are people who have divorced because of the type of spirits that lived in the buildings they rented.

I once visited a friend in his house, and it appeared all was well between him and his wife. I was watching TV in their living room the first night of my visit, and in the process I fell asleep. Somewhere in the middle of the night God opened my eyes, and I saw two other beings with me in the living room. They appeared to be men sitting on the sofa. I was shocked. I asked them, "What are you doing here? Where did you come from?"

"We have been in this house for a long time. This is our home. The couple came to meet us here," they replied. I inquired further who they were. "We are the spirits of divorce. As long as we are in this house, we will ensure that this couple divorces. We have been the cause of many divorces in this house."

I rebuked them in Jesus's name, and they took to their heels and fled.

The following day I questioned the couple about the state of their marriage, and they confessed it was in a bad shape. Their conduct toward each other was bad, their language was abusive, and there was tension in the house. It was so bad that they were even contemplating divorce.

Instantly I knew they were under a spiritual attack. I told them about my vision and prayed for them. I am happy to tell you that as I write this book, they are still happily married.

THE SPIRIT OF DIABETES

In a related story, a brother told me he bought a house that was once a place for old folks. He said after moving into the house, he slept one night and had a terrible spiritual attack. He said he felt an obscured figure enter him. Shortly after that, he developed diabetes.

What happened to him? Your guess is as good as mine.

YOUR CONDUCT CAN BE AFFECTED

When a spirit fills a house, it can fill the people living in the house in many ways. First of all, your conduct can be influenced.

In the Book of Acts, the people started walking and behaving like drunken men.

There are people whose behavior has changed radically after moving to a new area or home. This could be due to the influence of squatters. Nice respectful kids have been known to turn into monsters after changing homes.

Loving husbands have been known to turn into angry spouses after changing location. Squatters could be responsible.

YOUR EMOTIONS AND SPEECH CAN BE AFFECTED

Second, spirits can influence emotions and become very bold. Assuming the Holy Spirit is not present, can you imagine the negative emotions that can be stirred up? Resentment could replace tolerance. It is important for married couples to pray over houses they rent.

A spirit of resentment can cause you to resent your spouse and even your children. There are marital homes that are breeding grounds of evil spirits. The only marital quarrel I have found recorded in Scripture was between Job and his wife (Job 2:9-10). His wife wished him dead. He replied by calling her a foolish woman. This quarrel was orchestrated by demons that had infiltrated their home.

A demon of divorce occupying a home can collapse a harmonious marriage.

It is pretty serious if your wife recommends you die while she lives. It showed the extent to which their relationship had broken down. All these emotions were stirred up by demon activity.

Make sure you eject any spiritual squatter from any house you rent or build before you occupy it.

Let me ask you a question. Is your love for your spouse

or church fading? Pray about it. Do you have a shorter fuse of anger especially at home? Pray about it.

What lessons can we draw from this?

Every time I sleep outside my home, I make sure I sprinkle the blood of Jesus by confession. I pray and take spiritual control of the place and deploy angels to watch over me.

I believe that whenever you move into a new house, sleep in a hotel room, or sleep in someone's house, you should take spiritual control of that space because you do not know the spirits that were there before you came. The same applies to moving to a new office space.

You can lose every ounce of affection you have for your wife due to the influence of a squatter. May God open fresh love into your marriage, and I rebuke every squatter in Jesus's name!

Take Spiritual Control

When you are about to build a house, I believe you must pray over the land and displace all spiritual squatters before you proceed to build. I believe in taking spiritual control!

There are people who are sick because of the spirits that inhabit the place where they live. I believe there are businesses that are folding up because of the spirits that inhabit their offices and shops.

I also believe there are churches that are not growing because of the spirits that inhabit the city. Did you know that Satan had a seat in the city of Pergamos? God told the church at Pergamos, "I know thy works, and where thou dwellest, even where Satan's seat is: and thou holdest fast my name, and hast not denied my faith, even in those days wherein Antipas was my faithful martyr, who was slain among you, where Satan dwelleth" (Rev. 2:13).

Because of the spiritual presence of Satan himself in this city believers were being martyred.

THE CROCODILE IN THE CHURCH

One day God granted me a vision of the first church I pastored. In the vision there was a huge crocodile lying beneath the chairs of those seated to the right of the pulpit.

When I preached, the spirit either caused the people to sleep, be inattentive, or be spiritually deaf. Because of this, that section of the church was never full.

After the vision I prayed over that section of the church. Shortly after that, that section was filled to capacity. We even had to add more chairs.

You may not be able to take territorial control of the world, but you can take territorial control of your home, office, shop, and land.

It is up to you, now, to eject every spiritual squatter. The big question then is: What do we have to do concerning this threat?

The answer is simple! Let God arise on your behalf.

CHAPTER 7

LET GOD ARISE

> *Let God arise, let his enemies be scattered: let them also that hate him flee before him. As smoke is driven away, so drive them away: as wax melteth before the fire, so let the wicked perish at the presence of God.*
>
> —Psalm 68:1–2

THE WORD *LET* means to make something possible through a specific action.

According to this psalm, the presence of God can be released into a place. God is waiting for us to initiate the move to make Him rise to our defense. If God does not arise, the failure will not be His but ours. When God arises, His enemies will definitely scatter.

Symbols of the Spirit

The first symbol used to depict God's enemies, which includes demons, is the symbol of *smoke*. Smoke pollutes the air. Another symbol that is used is the symbol of *wax*.

The Holy Spirit is symbolized as wind or fire. On the Day of Pentecost the Holy Spirit came in as wind and fire.

> And suddenly there came a sound from heaven as a rushing *mighty wind*, and it filled all the house where they were sitting and there appeared unto them cloven tongues like *fire* and it sat upon each of them.
> —Act 2:2–3, emphasis added

It is interesting to note that the fire and the wind appeared and filled the house where they were sitting. The wind can quickly dispel smoke or a polluted environment, while fire can melt wax easily without stress. This is illustrative of the ease with which the Spirit of God can drive out demons; the Spirit of God can easily dismiss any demonic presence.

Stand Up and Be Counted

I am not asking you to move from your house. What I am asking you to do is to take territorial control of where you live or work by introducing the presence of the Holy Spirit. You do not have to move; it is the demons that have to move.

I pray that the fire and the wind of the Holy Spirit will fill your house!

Recently I heard a story that made me sad. A woman told me her parents had moved in with her. When I probed further, she told me they had moved from their house to move in with her because they believed their house was being haunted. Demons had chased them out!

The opposite must happen. We must rather chase out Satan and his cohorts.

THE CAT AND THE MICE

"When the cat's away, the mice will play."

One day I heard a noise coming from my attic. I could hear a lot of scampering. Immediately I knew that I had squatters (mice) in my house. They were not paying rent or helping to pay the bills, but they had moved in with me. I reflected on how best to deal with this menace. After careful thought, I decided to buy a cat and put it in the attic every evening.

From the day I introduced the cat into the attic, I did not hear from the mice again. They all ran away.

The time has come for the "big cat," the Lion of the tribe of Judah, to arise for all demonic presence to disappear. Let God arise and let His enemies be scattered.

One big question that faces us now is, "What do we do for God to come to our defense?" I believe there are several ways, but I want to share with you one way.

HOW TO EXERCISE POWER

One way you can release the presence of God is through *the anointing oil and prayer.*

The anointing oil is symbolic of the Holy Spirit. The word *symbol* means something visible, which by association or convention represents something else that is invisible. The Holy Spirit, being a spirit, is invisible.

When the anointing oil is applied by prayer through faith, it releases the presence and power of the Holy Spirit.

PRAYER, FAITH, AND THE ANOINTING OIL RELEASE POWER

Prayer, faith, and the anointing oil can release the presence of God into the atmosphere.

I will use two scriptures, one from the Old Testament and another from the New Testament, to clarify this statement.

> And thou shalt make it an oil of holy ointment, an ointment compound after the art of the apothecary: it shall be an holy anointing oil. And thou shalt anoint the tabernacle of the congregation therewith, and the ark of the testimony, and the table and all his vessels, and the candlestick and his vessels, and the altar of incense.... And thou shalt anoint Aaron and his sons, and consecrate them, that they may minister unto me in the priest's office.
> —Exodus 30:25–30

In Exodus 25 God instructed Moses to turn ordinary oil into anointing oil. I find the opening statement interesting. He said, "Thou shall make it an oil of holy ointment," or a holy anointing oil. God put the power to transform ordinary oil into supernatural anointing oil, in the hands of Moses.

You can buy ordinary olive oil and turn it into something supernatural by prayer and faith. Amen!

> Is any sick among you? Let him call for the elders of the church; and let them pray over him, anointing him with oil in the name of the Lord: And the prayer of faith shall save the sick, and the Lord shall raise him up; and if he have committed sins, they shall be forgiven him.
> —James 5:14–15

According to this verse, if anyone was sick in the church, one channel of divine healing was to pray over him, anointing him with oil in faith.

THE ANOINTING OIL RELEASES THE PRESENCE AND POWER OF GOD

The effect of this act is what intrigues me: "The Lord shall raise him up."

Here, the oil and prayer were expected to release the very presence of the Lord. The Lord then would proceed to raise the sick from his sickbed. The anointing oil releases the presence of God, hallelujah!

Another thing we can learn from Scripture is that the anointing oil can be applied on objects and buildings. Moses was asked to anoint the tabernacle (which was a building) and the vessels. The aim was to consecrate them.

One definition of the word *consecrate* is to dedicate something to a deity by a vow. Anything the oil touched was to be God's property.

The anointing oil also helps us to relinquish ownership and surrender things to God. When demons pass by, they see the seal of God and the Holy Spirit on the doors, and they run in terror.

We are told in Ephesians 1:13 that the Holy Spirit is the seal of God. One definition of the word *seal* is an official mark on a document, sometimes made with wax, which shows that it is legal or has been officially approved.

Believers are sealed with the Spirit, as God's mark put upon them.

Sometimes I see the seal of security companies on the gates of the property they protect. The seal is to remind you that although you may not see anyone around, there is a whole security apparatus protecting those properties. In case you wanted to break in, you would not have to deal with the owner; you would have to deal with trained and armed security men.

The oil of God upon your door will work like the blood that Moses smeared on the houses of the Israelites in Egypt. The blood gave them a superior status and delivered them from the angel of death. We read that by morning all the firstborn babies in Egypt, from the king to the maidservant and to beasts, had all died. The blood granted the people of Israel immunity.

If you own valuables, you can determine their level of security and protection by what you do. A dog in the White House may be far safer from terrorists than ordinary human beings walking on the streets. It may be an ordinary dog, but I tell you if it is the property of the American president, it will be far safer from attack than many other US citizens.

If a dog in the White House is that secure, can you imagine how secure your house will be when God becomes the owner of the house?

May the power of prayer and the anointing oil do the same for you. Amen!

It Caught Fire

One day during an anointing service I prayed over a bottle of oil and gave it to a certain woman. After the service she anointed her house by sprinkling the oil on the walls. The following day the house caught fire.

Unfortunately, her bedridden grandmother was in the house alone when it happened. Her whole room got burnt, but the fire never got to the bed. It became an island in the middle of the ashes. She was asleep while all this was going on. I believe the presence of God protected her.

THE MEASUREMENT OF POWER

How powerful are prayers and the anointing oil? How can it be measured? I will share with you a letter I received from a brother about the power of the anointing oil.

> Dear Prophet,
>
> I am very grateful to our Lord and Savior, Jesus Christ, for using you to transform my own life and so many others around the world.
>
> In fact, I do not know how to summarize this testimony, but I will try my best.
>
> You preached on a series titled, "The Unlawful Tenant." During the course of the series you told the congregation to bring some anointing oil for prayer. After your prophetic message, you told us to lift our oils, and you prayed a powerful prophetic prayer on them. You told us to anoint our houses, offices, and cars.
>
> You also prophesied that if we anointed our buildings that very night, God will reveal things to us spiritually. When I went home, I anointed my house and compound.
>
> Afterward, I decided to visit a friend who was sick. I had barely been away for three minutes when my wife called and told me three bats had appeared in our bedroom after applying the oil. She said they had even tried to sit on her head. I quickly rushed home, picked up a broom, and used it to kill one of the bats. I then tossed it into a fire.
>
> To my surprise, the bat resurrected and flew from the fire. I fought with these three bats for almost two hours. Afterward, we prayed and went to sleep. Then I had a dream. In this dream I saw myself sitting around a table with two other men in my house.

One of the men was short and had a white beard. He said to me, "No one has ever lived in this house for a long period, apart from you." I told him to leave in Jesus' name, and I saw him running out of the house with the other man following.

Immediately my eyes opened, and I found myself in my bed. I prayed until daybreak. The next morning when I went to my living room, I saw three extra dead bats lying on the floor. The Lord had executed them at night. I bowed my head and gave thanks to Jesus. After this incident, I was sharing with my wife one night what had happened. We did not go to sleep early. At midnight, we heard a noise like the cry of a crow on top of our roof. I went out to see what it was but did not find anything.

When I got back to my bedroom, my wife with whom I had been having fellowship a few minutes before was dying on the bed. My wife was dying. I called her, but she would not respond. I shook her, but she was lifeless.

Then I remembered the anointing oil you had prayed over. I splashed some on her. Instantly she opened her eyes. An evil spirit manifested and said to me, "Unless Pastor Baiden himself comes to pray, I will not go." I then knew this was a demonic attack. After a little more prayer and application of the anointing oil, the evil spirit left her.

Prophet, she is well now, but as long as the evil spirit mentioned your name, I want to bring her for another touch. I thank the Lord Jesus for delivering us. Praise unto His holy name!

Yours in Christ.

Psalm 89:20–23 gives us an idea of the effect of the anointing oil; these were the spiritual implications when the anointing oil was rubbed on David.

> I have found David my servant; with my holy oil have I anointed him: With whom my hand shall be established: mine arm also shall strengthen him. The enemy shall not *exact* upon him; nor the son of wickedness afflict him. And I will *beat down* his foes before his face, and plague them that hate.
> —Emphasis added

When you pray and rub the anointing oil upon your building, you will produce the same effect. Let's look at that scripture in detail. I would like you to highlight verses 22 and 23.

God said the first effect of the anointing oil was that no enemy will be able to *exact* upon him. The word *exact* means to claim as due or just.

There is no demon that can stake any claim to your land after the anointing oil has been applied. In Job 1:10, Satan went complaining to God that He had built a spiritual wall around Job's house. "Has thou not made a hedge about him, and about his house, and about all that he has on every side?"

The second effect was, God was going to give His enemies a sound beating. May God give all your spiritual enemies a sound beating! Amen! "Having spoiled principalities and powers, he made a shew of them openly, triumphing over them in it" (Col. 2:15).

I see peace come to your home! God will save you from divorce, He will save your children from drugs, and He will keep you safe from disease, in the mighty name of Jesus! Amen!

SQUATTERS

Maybe as you are reading, you are wondering what you can do to drive out squatters from your house. Do you have a bottle of anointing oil?

I would advice you to go get one if you do not have one.

CHAPTER 8

LET US PRAY

> For he hath broken the gates of brass, and cut the bars of iron in sunder....Then they cry unto the Lord in their trouble, and he saveth them out of their distresses. He sent his word, and healed them, and delivered them from their destructions.
> —Psalm 107:16, 19–20

PRAY THIS PRAYER below aloud in faith. God will hear you. After this prayer, anoint your house and behold the glory and wonders of God.

Today, as you pray over this oil, something is going to happen. If you are broke, you will never become broke again! If you cannot give birth, you are about to have your firstborn child! If you are always sick, you are going to be perpetually healed! All you need is faith.

When the anointing oil hits your bedroom, your kitchen, your garage, your car, or your walls, something will happen. The same thing that happened to David in Psalm 89:20–23, will happen to you. Amen!

SQUATTERS

This prayer is about to transform the oil into a holy anointing oil that carries the presence of God.

Shall we pray:

> *Father, in the name of Jesus, I call upon the Holy Ghost fire that fell on the Day of Pentecost to fall upon this anointing oil.*
>
> *I pray that the presence of Your Spirit will infuse this bottle. I pray, God, that every drop of oil will be saturated with Your presence. For You said to Moses, "Turn it into an holy anointing oil." And today in prayer, I turn it into an holy anointing oil, in the name of Jesus. And I pray, God, that it shall be a witness in the realm of the Spirit wherever I apply it.*
>
> *When I apply it in my home, my office, my shop, and on my car, let God arise and let His enemies be scattered. I pray, God, according to Your Word, that the enemy will not EXACT upon me, nor will the son of wickedness afflict me.*
>
> *I pray, God, that every yoke of bondage will be broken in the name of Jesus. Every spiritual squatter that lives in my home, that rules the atmosphere, that lives on my land, I pray, God, that this oil by Your Spirit, will EJECT any such spirit, in the name of Jesus.*
>
> *I pray, Lord, that You will BEAT DOWN every foe, for You have promised, "I will BEAT DOWN his foes before his face, and plague them that hate him." Plague my enemies. Let their way be dark and slippery. Let the angels of God persecute them.*

Let the whole army of heaven follow this anointing oil and enforce peace in my home.

Father, I pray for blessings, protection, prosperity, and peace to infuse this oil in the name of Jesus.

Your Word said, "Let the wicked perish at the presence of God." Wherever I sprinkle this oil, let the wicked perish.

Father, I say, hallowed be Thy name. I thank You for Your Word. I thank You that You have chosen the foolish things of this world to confound the wise. I thank You that the natural man cannot receive the things of the spirit. But we are spiritual people, and we thank You for spiritual truths, in the name of Jesus.

May I experience the protection, blessing, and prosperity of the almighty God, which passes all understanding.

Thank You in Jesus' name. Amen!

CHAPTER 9

REST ON EVERY SIDE

Thou knowest how that David my father could not build an house unto the name of the Lord his God for the wars which were about him on every side, until the Lord put them under the soles of his feet. But now the Lord my God hath given me rest on every side, so that there is neither adversary nor evil occurrent.

—1 Kings 5:3–4

Once we have completely ejected the squatter from our homes, offices, shops, and lives by the use of the anointing oil in prayer through faith, what is left for us to do is to maintain the peace.

Maintaining the Peace

After every major conflict or war, one thing that is required is the maintenance of peace, law, and order. After America won the war in Iraq, one major hurdle they faced was how to maintain peace. It is one thing to be victorious, but another to maintain peace.

Every good thing has to be maintained. Riches have to be maintained, anointing has to be maintained, and God's presence has to be maintained.

Solomon has a solemn warning for all of us.

> Be thou diligent to know the state of thy flocks, and look well to thy herds. For riches are not for ever: and doth the crown endure to every generation?
> —Proverbs 27:23–24

Let me remind you of the story of the prodigal son. We recall that after taking his share of the wealth, he could not maintain it.

> And when he had spent all, there arose a mighty famine in that land; and he began to be in want.
> —Luke 15:14

Again, a good marriage has to be maintained. You may have a marriage ceremony with a pink wedding dress, a huge cake, seventeen flower girls all in pink, and have a wonderful ceremony. And there is nothing necessarily wrong with that if you can afford it, but after all the fanfare, remember, that it is a lifetime commitment and has to be maintained.

Sometimes we service and maintain our cars more than our lives. Even your health has to be maintained.

The Example of Solomon

When Solomon took over as king of Israel, the whole kingdom was at rest because David, his father, had subdued all the enemies of Israel. This is part of a message he sent to Hiram.

> Thou knowest how that David my father could not build a house unto the name of the Lord his God for the wars which were about him on every side, until the Lord put them under the soles of his feet. But now the Lord my God hath given me rest on every side, so that there is neither adversary nor evil occurrent.
>
> —1 Kings 5:3–4

Solomon, however, could not maintain the peace because his heart departed from the Lord. Many enemies arose against him, and eventually the kingdom was divided in two during the reign of Rehoboam.

It is one thing to secure victory, and another to maintain peace. This natural truth has a reflection in the spirit realm.

One day Jesus healed a man who was afflicted with a dumb spirit. When the spirit left, the man spoke. The Pharisees accused Jesus of doing miracles with the power of the devil. Jesus went on to explain what happens when an unclean spirit leaves a man.

> When the unclean spirit is gone out of a man, he walketh through dry places, seeking rest; and finding none, he saith, I will return unto my house whence I came out. And when he cometh, he findeth it swept and garnished. Then goeth he, and taketh to him seven other spirits more wicked than himself; and they enter in, and dwell there: and the last state of that man is worse than the first.
>
> —Luke 11:24–26

It is clear from this scripture that it is not enough to drive demons away. We must also maintain the peace;

otherwise, the situation could get worse. When demons leave a place, they will launch repeated attacks to get back.

When a man is set free from demonic harassment, he has a responsibility to ensure that the demons do not return.

The mistake we make is that we free ourselves of all responsibility and make God and the pastor, who probably prayed for us, solely responsible. After the ejection exercise, you have a responsibility to maintain the peace.

The demon found two conditions prevailing; it was empty and no one was there. The Holy Spirit should have been there, but He was not there. Why? Because this person could not maintain his healing.

Have you noticed that when you build a house and do not move inside, squatters (snakes, lizards, mice, etc.) may make it their home? There is a cliché that goes, "Nature abhors a vacuum." It is true!

The house was garnished or decorated. The prevailing conditions suited the demons. Sin will only create a good atmosphere for demonic activity. Be holy and live for the Lord.

Obadiah 17 says, "But upon mount Zion shall be deliverance, and there shall be holiness; and the house of Jacob shall possess their possessions."

After deliverance, there must be a commitment to holiness, to maintain what was lost.

We Have a Responsibility

One day I received a phone call from a pastor in another town. He told me a member of his congregation had developed schizophrenia, and it was so severe that the person could not even remember her name. He informed me that while praying for her, the Lord told him to bring the lady to me for prayer and He would heal her. Since I had a witness in my spirit and he told me it was a direction from the Lord, I agreed.

When they came, I asked this demon-possessed lady what her name was. The only reply I received was a loud shriek. After praying for her and wrestling in prayer with these demons, the lady was completely healed and regained soundness of mind. We were all overjoyed with what Jesus had done.

Three weeks after the incident, the demons returned. She developed schizophrenia again.

They came again for prayer, and again the demons were driven out and she was healed.

This cycle occurred a third time. I asked the Lord why that problem kept on recurring. His answer was this scripture—Luke 11:24-26.

The spirits always returned because her heart was empty of the Spirit of God and the Word of God. After praying the third time and delivering her, I asked her to move to our town because I wanted to help her get established in the Word of God after her deliverance. This time around the demons never returned again, and she maintained her deliverance.

In Luke 4:13 we see from the temptation of Jesus that the devil left Him for a season. This means that the devil came back to launch another attack. That is why it is possible to lose your healing even after you have been delivered.

Do you remember that when Jesus healed a lame man in John 5, He cautioned him about maintaining his healing? He said, "Afterward Jesus findeth him in the temple, and said unto him, Behold, thou art made whole: sin no more, lest a worse thing come unto thee" (John 5:14).

Can you imagine that even though he had been healed

by Jesus Himself, the responsibility to maintain his healing was still his? We must make it a point, then, to maintain whatever form of healing we would receive.

The Holy Spirit Helps Maintain the Peace

The presence of the Holy Spirit helps maintain peace.

I used to have a very wild dog in my house. Because of the presence of this vicious dog, anytime my friends came to visit me they would ask whether the dog was bound before entering my house. They wanted to check out who was there. Before Satan and his cohorts visit you, they always want to find out who is there. Is it your boyfriend, your sister, or brother-in-law? Who is there? Is it God?

In the Book of Job, Satan told the Lord he had been visiting many homes without any restrictions. The only home he had not been able to visit was Job's home. Satan could not visit Job's house because the Lord was there. Is God in your house?

Satan said, "Hast thou not made an hedge about him, and about his house, and about all that he hath on every side?" (Job 1:10).

This scripture became very clear to me as a result of a vision I had one day.

A Vision About Protection

In this vision I was in a car driving home. When I got to my gate, I realized the whole house was surrounded by a steel wall.

I thought to myself, "Who came to build this steel wall around my house?"

Upon careful inspection, I realized there was no opening

into the house. It was one homogenous wall without a line. I started thinking, "How can I go home?"

As soon as the thought came into me, the wall separated, and an avenue was created for me to drive through. On my way I realized I was not home yet. There was yet another steel wall. This also opened for me to drive through. After this, there was a third wall, which also separated to allow me through. It was then that I saw the driveway to my house.

The Lord said to me in the vision, "I am watching over you."

This always makes me appreciate the three walls God built around Job's house. God built a wall around Job, around his house, and around everything he had.

These are the three walls.

In Psalm 23 David, who was used to danger, expressed the source of his security. "I will fear no evil: for thou art with me" (Ps. 23:4).

May God protect your house today and always. Amen! How can He protect your house?

CHAPTER 10

HOSTING THE HOLY SPIRIT

But upon mount Zion shall be deliverance, and there shall be holiness; and the house of Jacob shall possess their possessions.
—Obadiah 17

One of the things that represent the Holy Spirit is the dove. This dove will hover and land in your house under the right conditions. It landed on Jesus and remained on Him.

It never left Him because Jesus was able to maintain His presence. How did He do that?

The Dove Hovers Over Lambs

What makes one maintain the presence of the Holy Spirit? It is one's nature.

In order to maintain the presence of the Holy Spirit in our lives, we must have the nature of the lamb. Spiritually, Jesus had the nature of a lamb, and that was why He was able to maintain His presence.

> The next day John seeth Jesus coming unto him and saith, Behold *the Lamb of God*, which taketh away the sin of the world! This is he of whom I said, After me cometh a man which is preferred before me: for he was before me. And I knew him not: but that he should be made manifest to Israel. Therefore am I come baptizing with water. And John bare record, saying, I saw the spirit descending from heaven like a dove, and it abode upon him. And I knew him not: but he that sent me to baptize with water, the same said unto me, Upon whom thou shalt see *the Spirit descending*, and remaining on him, the same is he which baptizeth with the Holy Ghost. And I saw, and bare record that this is the Son of God.
> —JOHN 1:29–34, EMPHASIS ADDED

The Holy Spirit remains over lambs. If you have the nature of a serpent, chicken, or a goat, He will not remain. That is why you must be a lamb in order to maintain the presence.

When John the Baptist saw the Pharisees, he did not see the nature of the lamb. He saw vipers. I wonder what creature your nature represents in the spirit.

What the Lamb Stands For

The lamb stands for two things: purity and meekness.

Purity

In the Old Testament the lamb was a symbol of purity. That was why it was mostly used as a sacrifice to God. If we intend on maintaining the Holy Spirit, we have to be pure; we must live holy lives.

We cannot continue to be liars and maintain His presence. Fornication and adultery will scare Him. Strife and pornography will scare Him. We cannot afford to have marital strife and live in a cold war for three weeks. Something higher is at stake.

The psalmist said, "I will wash my hands in innocency: so will I compass thine altar, O Lord" (Ps. 26:6).

David is saying, "I cannot live in Your presence if I do not sanctify myself."

He knew he could not be entertained around the altar if he was not clean.

> This then is the message which we heard of Him, and declare unto you, that God is light, and in him is no darkness at all. If we say that we have fellowship with him, and walk in darkness, we lie, and do not the truth: but if we walk in the light, as he is in the light, we have fellowship one with another, and the blood of Jesus Christ his Son cleanseth us from all sin.
> —1 John 1:5–7

Most of the time, to have fellowship with people, there must be a level of commonality: doctors fellowship together, artists fellowship together, etc.

I once went to a place called *Lions Park* in South Africa. As I observed the lions from a distance, they looked very cuddly and tame as the cubs lay on their mother and their whole pride huddled together. I wondered how nice it would be to cuddle with her. I knew, however, that I could not fellowship with them because I was not a lion.

To be able to fellowship with light, you must *be* light, as Paul wrote in 2 Corinthians 6:14: "Be ye not unequally yoked together with unbelievers: for what fellowship hath righteousness with unrighteousness? and what communion hath light with darkness?"

In order to have fellowship with God or be able to walk

closely with Him, we must walk in the light. God cannot be around you when you walk in darkness.

Nowadays, when I look at Christians, I am not sure what to think. People are in the church but are doing all manner of things. They are not married, yet they can afford to fornicate. They are businessmen but cannot afford to be truthful, and so on.

The Holy Spirit cannot be upon such persons. Sin repulses the presence of God.

Deuteronomy 23:14 says, "For the Lord thy God walketh in the midst of thy camp, to deliver thee…therefore shall thy camp be holy: that he see no unclean thing in thee, and turn away from thee."

This means that God detests sin, but holiness, on the other hand, will entertain Him. Many of us are not aware that once we walk in holiness, we are automatically protected. In the story of Job, his protection was as a result of his holiness. "There was a man in the land of Uz, whose name was Job; and that man was perfect and upright, and one that feared God, and eschewed evil" (Job 1:1).

A Dangerous Sin

> But he that hateth his brother is in darkness, and walketh in darkness, and knoweth not whither he goeth, because that darkness hath blinded his eyes.
> —1 John 2:11

One of the most dangerous sins that can take us out of fellowship with God is unforgiveness. It plunges you into darkness.

My experience

One day a brother did something to me, and I was not happy with it. I decided to stay cordial with him.

Most of us take that stance and say, "I have forgiven him, but he does not have to be my friend." We must be careful, because mentally we can forgive someone, but in the depth of our hearts, we may not have done it.

Later on I had a vision about this whole thing. In the vision I had been taken away from the presence of God and locked up in a cell with hardened criminals. I could not believe it. The jailor said to me, "You are a pastor and do not belong here. But you are also here because you did not forgive Brother So-and-So. Because of that, you have been removed from the presence of God." I begged for forgiveness and pledged to take away every bitterness from my heart. Then and only then was I released.

Friend, unforgiveness between spouses will damage their fellowship with God. If you have not spoken to your wife for three days, now is the time to bring the glory back. If you have something against your parents, forgive them and entertain the Holy Spirit.

Holiness will keep you close to God.

MEEKNESS

The next characteristic of the dove is *meekness*. Some people disregard meekness and see it as a sign of weakness. In their opinion the description of a meek person is someone who is weak-willed and pushed around by everyone. That is far from it. Jesus was meek, but the Pharisees were not pushing Him around.

This is a scriptural meaning of meekness.

> The meek will he guide in judgment: and the meek will he teach his way.
>
> —Psalm 25:9

There are two things that distinguish the spiritually meek. They are *guidable* and *teachable*.

Let me ask you a question, "Are you guidable?" When you were getting married, did you rely on God to guide you through His Word? Did His Spirit make a judgment on whom you should marry? Are you fulfilling the call of God upon your life?

I want to ask again, "Are you teachable?" Who teaches you how to manage your money? Is it God or what you think? God teaches the meek on how to manage everything, including their money.

Who is teaching you how to relate to your spouse and children? Is it your mind or the Word of God? A teachable spirit relies on the Bible as a manual for his life.

Listen, the time for playing games is over. The night is far spent, and the day has come.

Let's open up our hearts and follow the Word of God. Let us be guidable, let us be teachable, and I tell you one thing, the Holy Spirit will always remain on you.

I believe I have put into your heart a key that the devil will not like you to know. The time has come for you to drive out every spiritual squatter from your environment. Step up and take control in Jesus' name.

It is my prayer that you will find rest on every side like in the days of Solomon.

> Thou knowest how that David my father could not build an house unto the name of the Lord his God

for the wars which were about him on every side, until the Lord put them under the soles of his feet.
—1 Kings 5:3

And Judah and Israel dwelt safely, every man under his vine and under his fig tree, from Dan even to Beersheba, all the days of Solomon.
—1 Kings 4:25

ABOUT KAKRA BAIDEN

MANY YEARS AGO, the Lord Jesus Christ appeared in a vision to Kakra Baiden and called him into the ministry as a prophet, teacher, and miracle worker. He is also known as *the walking Bible* for his supernatural ability to preach and teach the Bible from memory.

He is an architect by profession, and serves as a member of the bishops' council of the Lighthouse Chapel International denomination.

He has trained many pastors and ministers, and planted over fifty churches within the Lighthouse denomination.

Currently, he is the Senior Pastor of the Morning Star Cathedral, Lighthouse Chapel International.

He is also the president of Air Power Ministries, an interdenominational ministry that propagates the Word through conferences, radio, TV, and Internet to a global audience.

He is a sought-after revivalist and conference speaker, and the author of the best-selling book, *Squatters*.

He is married to Ewuradwoa Baiden and they have four children: Phoebe, Caleb, Joshua, and Chloe.

CONTACT THE AUTHOR

For additional information on Kakra Baiden's books, and messages (CDs & DVDs), write to any of these addresses:

United States:
26219 Halbrook Glen Lane
Katy, TX 77494

United Kingdom:
32 Tern Road
Hampton, Hargate
Cambridgeshire
Pe78DG

E-Mail:
info@kakrabaiden.org

Website:
www.kakrabaiden.org
http://www.facebook.com/kakrabaiden
www.twitter.com/ProphetKakraB

www.ingramcontent.com/pod-product-compliance
Lightning Source LLC
Chambersburg PA
CBHW071623040426
42452CB00009B/1462

A Note From Denise Renner

The Word of God is so powerful in our lives. It is essential that every person spend time with God and study His Word in order to stay spiritually strong in these last days.

This study guide corresponds to my *TIME With Denise Renner* TV program by the same title that can be viewed at **deniserenner.org**. My desire is that through these lessons, you find the encouragement and freedom in Christ that you need. I believe the Holy Spirit is going to speak to you through the words you read in this study tool and that as you begin to use it, you will be *propelled* into the abundant life God has planned for you. I encourage you to make the effort to receive all He has for you and all He wants to do in you — it will definitely be worth it!

Whether you have walked with the Lord a long time or have just begun to follow Him, there is so much He wants to give you from His Word. He sees where you are, and He wants to meet you there.

> Therefore do not worry about tomorrow, for tomorrow
> will worry about its own things.
> Sufficient for the day is its own trouble.
> — Matthew 6:34

Your sister and friend in Jesus Christ,

Denise Renner

Denise Renner

Unless otherwise indicated, all scripture quotations are taken from the *New King James Version*®. Copyright © 1982 by Thomas Nelson. Used by permission. All rights reserved.

Scripture quotations marked (*AMPC*) are taken from the *Amplified® Bible, Classic Edition*. Copyright © 1954, 1958, 1962, 1964, 1965, 1987 by The Lockman Foundation. Used by permission. **www.Lockman.org**.

Scripture quotations marked (*KJV*) are taken from the *King James Version* of the Bible.

Priceless! The Infinite Value of a Proverbs 31 Woman

Copyright © 2024 by Denise Renner
1814 W. Tacoma St.
Broken Arrow, Oklahoma 74012-1406

Published by Rick Renner Ministries
www.renner.org

ISBN 13: 978-1-6675-0642-5

eBook ISBN 13: 978-1-6675-0643-2

All rights reserved. No portion of this book may be reproduced or transmitted in any form or by any means — electronic, mechanical, photocopy, recording, scanning, or other (except for brief quotations in critical reviews or articles) — without the prior written permission of the Publisher.